GAGGED

GAGGED:

The 10 Mistakes That Stop Women From Being Heard At Work

By

Cynthia Leeds Friedlander

The examples in this book represent a range of situations and personalities. They are representative and stand for no specific actual individuals. The author cannot be held responsible for any interpretation or use of the book's content, suggestions and recommendations.

This material may not be duplicated or transmitted in any form without written permission of the author.

Copyright © 2018

All rights reserved.

ISBN: 978-0-9899536-1-0

Visit TodaysEmpoweredWoman.com to order books

To contact the author for coaching, workshops, and/or consulting: TodaysEmpoweredWoman.com

To listen to excepts of a conversation with the author about *GAGGED*, go to:
TodaysEmpoweredWoman.com

Dedication

I dedicate this book to Jill, the avatar for GAGGED. Jill is the synthesis of the hundreds of working women I've coached. She is my inspiration and my cause.

And to Karen and Steve Dimmick, who gave birth to GAGGED. Without their direction, I would have never written this book. Without their listening to me and really hearing me, GAGGED would have never come to be.

GAGGED:

The 10 Mistakes That Stop Women From Being Heard At Work

CONTENTS

Welcome to GAGGED..9
Jill: A New Leader's Struggle...13

1. The Good Girl and the Cookie..17
2. The Impossible Ideal..31
3. The Syndrome of Apology..39
4. Mechanics of Whining..47
5. Forgetting to Listen..57
6. Conscientiousness to the Extreme.....................................67
7. The Imposition of Standards..77
8. The Vicious Cycle: Feedback, Guilt, and Defensiveness.....89
9. Attachment to the Personal...97
10. The Voice of Authority...109

Jill: It's a New Day...121
The Guiding Principles for a Successful Life..........................125

Chapter Keys Review..127
Reminders Review...131

Welcome to GAGGED

Welcome! I'm so happy you've joined the conversation. That's the way I see GAGGED. As you're reading it, I want it to feel like we're in my living room in my house in upstate New York, sitting around the stone fireplace with a roaring fire and a big pot of hot chocolate (tea, coffee...) warming us as we examine and chat about the many facets of female endeavor and progress. I have so much I want to share with you. I've been coaching, counseling, and listening to you for many years and have been devoted to providing you with meaningful expertise, guidelines, perspectives, nuances, and tricky traps-to-avoid.

Destiny

One night when I was in graduate school, getting my Masters in Counseling from Hunter College in New York City, an adored professor announced at the beginning of class that there was an available internship for a program for women exploring re-entry into the workforce after staying home devoted to raising their children.

Before applying to grad school, I'd lived in the Bahamas for 18 months, dedicated to my little son, while my husband was on a work assignment. Shortly before we were scheduled to return to New York, I sent for applications to graduate schools. I'd been toying with going back to school since the birth of my son.

As the applications arrived, I stuffed them all in an empty kitchen drawer without opening them. It felt ominous to be thinking of going back to school ten years after earning my B.A. in French. When I finally gathered them up and opened one, the first thing that fell out of the envelope was an assortment of papers enfolded in a page with big letters that said:

GRE APPLICATION

I immediately took those loose papers and the unopened envelopes and stuffed them in the trash. Out of sight, out of mind. As much as I loved puzzles, riddles, quizzes, exams and tests of any kind – I'd always enjoyed figuring things out without help or clues – there was no way I wanted to take the Graduate Record Exam! I was terrified.

About three hours later, I returned home from the beach, went to the trash and retrieved my graduate school application mail. After careful examination, I discovered that the Masters in Counseling program I wanted to enroll in did not require the GRE. What a relief.

A year later, I sat on the edge of my seat, waiting for that night's class to be over so I could be the first student to inquire about the internship to support women considering re-entry into the workforce. For the next 12 years I was first an intern for and then the Coordinator of The Ellen Morse Tishman Memorial Seminars at Hunter College, City University of New York. I cut my teeth and honed my skills, working with hundreds of women there who were examining options and making choices for their next career and life steps.

If I hadn't retrieved the mail from the trash, if I hadn't been in that class that night, it's unlikely I would have started writing GAGGED or be sitting here at my laptop welcoming you into this conversation.

Many years have passed since grad school and many experiences have filled those years. I've developed a few areas of expertise including leadership, teambuilding, career management, and my main professional passion, communication effectiveness. I've worked for top-level outplacement and management consulting firms. I've had my own consulting and coaching practice. I've been an instructor in continuing education and graduate school programs. I've directed the Career Services department for a university and for a psychotherapy institute. I've had phenomenal corporate clients including Disney ABC, Time Warner Cable, Deutsche Bank, Harpo Productions, The National Trust for Historic Preservation, and NATO's Joint Forces Training Centre in Bydgoszcz, Poland. I've written prior books including *SPEAK EASY: The Communication Guide for Career and Life Success*.

The professional culmination of my career is *GAGGED: The 10 Mistakes That Stop Women From Being Heard At Work*. It's the embodiment of all my experience. Writing it has taken me back to that night I sat on the edge of my seat in that classroom, feeling destiny calling me and knowing I would be supporting women who want to contribute to the world through meaningful endeavors that match who they are as women and contribute to their personal definition of success.

This is for you! Welcome!

> **Let's begin with Jill. She's struggling with many challenges at work and at home. The pressures are mounting and she feels constricted, as if she's been GAGGED.**
>
> **Jill represents many women who are finding their way.**

A New Leader's Struggle

Jill is a 29-year-old project leader in a large financial technology firm. Her technology skills are stronger than her communication and interpersonal skills, although she gets along with everyone and is well liked.

She's been married for three years and is beginning to feel anxious about getting pregnant and juggling her career and her home life with a baby in the mix. She takes great pride in doing everything correctly so thinking about the right way of becoming a mother and building a family feels overwhelming. She is torn between being a loving wife and a potential nurturing mother while remaining a sharp, ambitious, successful, technology professional. Jill is accustomed to setting high standards and feels as if she's being pulled in impossible directions she'll never be able to achieve to her satisfaction.

She is a new team leader and is uncomfortable in her first position of authority with people who were peers up until now. Since she's so conscientious, Jill is concerned that people won't *like her anymore; she very much wants to be liked and craves the approval of others.*

She feels unsure of how to communicate with her new manager, Sarah, who is quite ambitious and critical. Sarah is a whip-cracker who wears blinders with only one focus: advancing her own career. Sarah rarely listens and only gives feedback that is project-related, unrealistically demanding, and negative. Jill wants to do the "right thing" for her manager yet feels a bit lost about how to accomplish that. She's always received lots of guidance and positive reinforcement from previous bosses and coworkers.

In reaction to her new manager's critical style, she always feels like she's doing everything wrong and, to make it even worse, she constantly feels guilty, even though she knows she's done nothing that merits guilt or apology. She can hear herself starting too many conversations with, "I'm sorry that…" and can't seem to get rid of this apologetic and self-demeaning approach. She's become aware of how whiney she sounds lately, has stopped leaving voicemail messages, and tries to write emails as much as possible to avoid direct conversations.

Jill is dedicatedly career-oriented and wants to do everything superbly. She vacillates between groveling and judging. Her insecurities and self-demands cause her to feel inadequate and her communication can sound pleading rather than authoritative. She keeps asking her team for "permission" rather than asserting her new leadership. In contrast, she also can sometimes sound harsh and critical. She is accustomed to doing everything herself "perfectly" and feels terrified that the mistakes or bad decisions her team makes will reflect on her, so she's having an extremely tough time coping when others don't do it "her way."

Jill knows that men intimidate her in her 80%-male work environment. Some of the intimidation is borderline sexual harassment. Some feels cultural; there is a global array of workers in the company, including many who have been raised with values and language where women are subjugated. Some is her "imagination." Most of it that matters comes from her inner conflict between being an accommodating, caring coworker and being a business-focused, professional colleague.

Things at home are tricky for Jill as well. Her communications are even becoming strained with her husband, Matt, who has always been her best friend and closest confidante. Matt keeps asking her, "What's wrong? We never talk anymore. You seem so closed off and shut down. How can I help?" Jill finds herself more resentful than appreciative of Matt and can't seem to open up with him. She can't understand where this is coming from or stop her new behavior and return to her former relaxed, casual, trusting way of communicating.

Jill decides she wants to search for something that will help her function better and reduce her anxiety. She has always loved identifying and purchasing self-help books geared to her needs. This time she can't quite figure out what specific help will make a difference.

- ➤ She's looking for a book with simple tools she can understand and apply right away.
- ➤ She's seeking help with the way she communicates.
- ➤ She wants a guide that comprehends what's going on internally with her emotions and reactions so she can manage her interactions with others more skillfully and professionally.
- ➤ She wants to know how to handle being a leader and a coworker simultaneously so she can build relationships at all levels.
- ➤ She'd like to feel the comfort level she always felt in the past with everyone at home and at work.

Jill finds "GAGGED: The 10 Mistakes That Stop Women From Being Heard At Work" and feels more at ease and confident with each page she reads.

🍪 The Good Girl and the Cookie

It's amazing to watch how hard and conscientiously women work, expecting reward and recognition to result automatically from their dedicated efforts. I've watched this for years and can feel myself wanting to shake those hard-working women by the shoulders and say, "Stop waiting for them to give you a cookie for your hard work! It's up to you to *ask* for the cookie. It's up to you to promote all that you're delivering and ask to be rewarded for your achieved results!"

After all, men come in asking for the cookie. They negotiate from the job interview to the job offer, from pay raise to pay raise, and from promotion to promotion. Men are usually less concerned about natural rewards accumulating in the background somewhere, based on how well they're doing their jobs. Instead, they stay focused on arranging every incentive possible for simply showing up.

I've coached numerous men and women and there's abundant overlap in their coaching needs. Along with multiple similarities, I've been struck by a significant distinguishing factor. Most of the men I coach keep their eye on the prize of achieving a promotion and a salary increase while most women focus on whether they're doing their job successfully enough to receive a promotion or a raise.

In the workplace, it's more likely a man will say, "Of course I can do that" - having never done "that" before. In the same situation, a woman is more likely to say, "I'm not sure I can do that" - since she's never done "that" before.

I label this distinction "The Good Girl and the Cookie."

Looking at a few of the basics of human development, we can easily understand the characteristics that contribute to this phenomenon.

We know the male is often driven to fix everything; it's his "mission." When he says, "I can do that" even though he never has, it comes from his drive to be "the fixer."

We see the female, who thrives on connection and relationships, often revealing trust and openness as her most fundamental drivers. When she says, "I don't know if I can do that" it's her determination to be open and honest, her priority of connection, that establishes the basis for her response.

These fundamentals set the stage for the Good Girl and the Cookie pattern. The little girl grows up wanting always to be the Good Girl. She learns, if she does *the right thing*, she'll get a cookie. She sets goals based on what being good means to her. She believes that being the Good Girl IS the ultimate objective. It becomes ingrained:

- Receiving the cookie comes from being good.
- The cookie is delicious.
- The cookie is desirable.
- The cookie is NOT the goal.
- Being GOOD is the goal.

So how can the Good Girl make asking for the cookie a natural and acceptable priority when her fundamental values are those just described?

There are five steps to becoming comfortable asking for rewards. The first step is to examine beliefs; the second step is to adjust perspectives; the third step is to ensure level communication; the fourth step is to identify tangible achievements and desired rewards; the fifth step is to continue the dialog:

1. Examine Beliefs

If we believe that asking for rewards or making rewards a priority is counter to our core values and to our ability to achieve success, we'll be reluctant to speak up and ask for what we desire. It's important to identify male and female role models who demonstrate solid ways of ensuring their progress and asking for what they want. When we can see people who are speaking up for themselves respectfully and successfully, it becomes easier to expand our beliefs and incorporate positive ways of asking for the rewards we merit.

A good way to look at your established view of the world is to write out some of your beliefs. If you're going to expand or adjust your views, make sure you have first identified and defined them clearly.

Here are examples of typical beliefs:

- "I believe that it's always better to let others praise me than to brag about my achievements."

> "I believe if I do a job well, people will notice and reward me for my good work."

> "I believe that people don't like those who are cocky and blow their own horn."

> "I believe that cream rises to the top; rewards come naturally to those who excel."

2. Adjust Perspectives

You may feel it's aggressive or arrogant to be self-promoting. To underscore the importance of expanding the way you perceive self-advancement, look again at those around you, male and female, who are strong self-promoters without being haughty or pushy. There are minor yet significant degrees of difference in these types of characteristics. Confident people are magnetic and attract others. Arrogant people are disliked and repel everyone. Watch out for claims of modesty as well. While modesty can be seen as the opposite of arrogance, and as a good quality, it can also be seen as lowly groveling. (More about groveling in The Syndrome of Apology chapter.)

The following chart breaks down these characteristics and points the way to adjusting your perspectives:

AVOID	IDEAL	AVOID
❦ Groveling	❦ Confident	❦ Arrogant
❦ Subservient	❦ Self-Assured	❦ Conceited
❦ Overly apologetic	❦ Assertive	❦ Big-Headed

Here are some adjusted perspectives to illustrate how beneficial it is to challenge your ingrained beliefs:

- **Former belief**: "I believe that it's always better to let others praise me than to brag about my achievements."
- **Adjusted perspective**: "I believe that confident people who enthusiastically and confidently describe their achievements are more likely to be rewarded than those who wait for others to recognize them.

- **Former belief**: "I believe if I do a job well, people will notice and reward me for my good work."
- **Adjusted perspective**: "I believe that simply doing a job well is less likely to win recognition than proactively presenting achievement."

- **Former belief**: "I believe that people don't like those who are cocky and blow their own horn."
- **Adjusted perspective**: "I believe that there's a big difference between being cocky and being confident and see the benefits that can be gained from the latter."

> **Former belief**: "I believe that cream rises to the top; rewards come naturally to those who excel."

> **Adjusted perspective:** "I believe that dedication to excellence is a good starting place and recognize that proactive goal setting and self-promotion are the keys to recognition and success."

3. Ensure Level Communication

We all know "It's not what you say; it's how you say it." Most of how communication is received is about tone and facial expression. The most important element in our communications is to keep the communication level. Think of the two-way street of equal communication, no matter the status of the other person in the dialog.

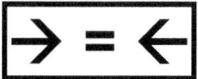

The internet and social media, accompanied by texting and email, have dramatically enhanced how we communicate. They have also contributed to the avoidance of direct communication even for communications that would be better spoken, face-to-face, or voice-to-voice in real time. People interpret what people say and what they write. These interpretations can be far from the intent of the communicator. Direct communication helps to limit misinterpretation.

4. Identify Tangible Achievements and Desired Rewards

Making a list of your achievements and contributions can be quite satisfying. Give yourself this gift and make the list full of self-recognition. If you decide to use the list in actual communications with your manager or other decision-makers, make sure the language shows your leadership and specific contributions while also emphasizing the related accomplishments of the team and other contributors. Use the word "we" extensively. Also, defining and mapping out the rewards you want will be critical to recognizing their validity and actually being able to ask for and gain them.

5. Continue the Dialog

These recommended adjustments must become incorporated into a new ongoing approach. A one-time attempt is unlikely to be enough to shift the playing field or gain the outcomes you want. People are used to you as the Good Girl who delivers much and asks for little. And it's human nature to return to old comfortable patterns. There's also a possibility, because this is new behavior or a different style of communication from what people are used to hearing, your delivery may be different from what you intend.

⚷ Reminder:

A coach, mentor, or prior coworker may be beneficial as you work on new communications. Feedback is always valuable. We cannot hear or see ourselves the way others do.

It may help you feel more comfortable making these requests if you think about the innocence of small children who always ask for what they want without hesitation, even after being refused multiple times. These conversations requesting recognition and reward are likely to go smoothly as long as you are illustrating strong contributions and making relevant requests and as long as your requests are presented without demand or ultimatum. There are many "cookies" you can ask for besides a salary increase or a job promotion.

Here are potential rewards (cookies) you may want to request:

- New office or work station location
- Enhancement of job title
- Adjustment of job description
- Inclusion in decision making groups
- Being featured in a newsletter or other publication
- Gaining or providing a mentoring relationship
- Additional staffing for mandates or benchmarks
- Participation in developing new policy
- Paid attendance for a class or conference
- Flexible work schedule
- Work from home hours
- Retreat budget for your team
- New technology to enhance or expedite work outcomes
- Gift rewards to recognize staff members

> 🔑 **Reminder:**
>
> *Make sure you link the rewards you're seeking to benefits to the company (such as boosting morale, increasing productivity, enhancing efficiency, achieving better results, and/or gaining dedication to standards).*

AVOID: "I'd like to have the title, Program Director, rather than Program Coordinator of this new department. I was a program coordinator in my prior job and I'll have much more responsibility in this new role. I'd really like the title of Program Director to show I'm at a higher level in my new job."

BETTER: "I'm excited about and eager to fulfill the demands and responsibilities of this new role. It will be important for me to have the title of Program Director to make sure the new department achieves the level of success we want. I'll be interacting with many senior executives who will be much more responsive and receptive to someone who has a title on their level. The right job title will contribute to people seeing the department as significant which is our goal. This is an important distinction for us to create for this upcoming program launch."

Present your story and your request, making sure you have incorporated these types of communications:

"Let's keep talking about this."

"I know we can agree about the best way to do this."

"When is the right time for me to circle back with you on this?"

"What would it take to get this accomplished?"

"How would you like for me to move this ahead?"

"Let's keep talking…"

There are vital elements, essential for beneficial conversations and fruitful outcomes.

Remember these **3 P**s and the fine lines that separate them:

- **P**leading is unappealing.
- **P**ersistence wins rewards.
- **P**ushiness repels.

It's valuable to think of the above five steps as authentic, proactive, enrichment tools for your beliefs and strengths. The goal is to fortify your ability to be heard and respected without giving up your core values or trying to twist yourself into a male pretzel version of some ineffective business stereotype. This is about good career management. This is *not* about being the Good Girl waiting for her cookie to be rewarded.

To receive detailed step by step Negotiation and Decision-Making grids to help you define your objectives and make better decisions, go to:
TodaysEmpoweredWoman.com/Be-Heard

🔑 The Good Girl and the Cookie

Keys to Becoming Un-Gagged

➤ Feedback is always valuable.

➤ Managing your career means being proactive.

➤ It's up to you to promote your accomplishments.

➤ Confidence is magnetic and attracts people to you.

➤ Taking initiative is as important as conscientiousness.

The Impossible Ideal

The Good Girl and the Cookie pattern is interwoven and reflected in surveys, repeated over the years, reflecting how women face certain self-identity challenges that men mostly do not experience.

The Checklist

In this revealing survey, people of diverse gender, age, and socio-economic backgrounds were given three pages of adjectives with checkboxes. Each of the pages contained an identical list of adjectives. There was a different instruction on each page:

> Page 1: Check the adjectives that describe the ideal female.
> Page 2: Check the adjectives that describe the ideal male.
> Page 3: Check the adjectives that describe the ideal successful professional person.

Each time the results were gathered, the findings were the same. The men (with or without jobs, young or old, rich or poor, educated or uneducated) saw the ideal male and the ideal successful professional person as one and the same. The women also checked the same boxes for the ideal male and the ideal successful professional person. When asked to check the adjectives that describe the ideal female, both men and women checked different boxes from those for the ideal male and ideal successful professional person.

When males assign descriptors to women that differentiate the ideal female from the ideal male, it presents zero conflict in the self-image of those men and possibly even heightens their sense of identity and strength. Men's sense of self may even be artificially heightened from these perceptions, causing potential condescension and sexism.

These views of success and the optimum male provide a basis for male self-identity, self-awareness and self-confidence that is defined and solid.

The female, in contrast, is left somewhat torn. What if she wants to be the ideal female – the Good Girl – as much as she wants to be the ideal successful professional? How can she combine these two easily if she, and the rest of the world, sees them at odds with each other? How can she succeed in embracing and desiring both?

If, for example, "nurturing" is one of the adjectives consistently checked for the ideal female (by both men and women) and is never checked for the ideal male nor the ideal successful professional person, there emerges a natural duality that a woman will experience that a man will not.

This duality is reflected in the ages-old debate: "You can have it all!" ... Can I? There are arguments on both sides. Ivanka Trump would argue that it's all about "architecting" your life. I would contend it may be tightly connected to financial circumstances. Having the funds for support services and domestic help can certainly alleviate some of the pressures of trying to achieve "having it all."

I see this duality as being more about the struggle to achieve the right balance between how a woman sees herself as a woman and how she sees herself as a professional woman in business. The duality comes down to how a woman views herself.

The adjective checklist exists in all of us in some hidden subconscious way. We've all created the boxes that make up our view of what's ideal. The only way to break out of the "ideal" trap is to change the adjectives we check for the ideal successful professional person.

⌛ **Reminder:**

> ***We must make sure we're striving for our own ideals and not those we're unconsciously brainwashed to fit into.***

Years ago, I attended a career planning seminar in New York City that included a guided visualization workshop. There was wonderful Yanni meditation music with relaxation guidance to take us to a transcendent introspective state. With our eyes closed and our shoes off, enveloped in pillows and blankets on the floor, we were guided through a day five years in the future. We were asked to visualize our entire day, starting with waking up in the morning. This was supposed to be a typical day in our everyday lives down the road.

California Dreaming

My day started out with seaside sunshine streaming in through ceiling-to-floor glass surrounded by 270 degrees of Pacific Ocean views. After breakfast, I sped down the 405 Freeway (with nearly zero traffic) in a convertible with the top down, wearing a full-length fur coat. (It may have been a Maserati and the fox fur I was wearing didn't match my value system or the 80-degree temperature of the California air.)

I felt completely comfortable and confident as I headed to work. I parked my car and arrived at another glass-walled space. I walked into my corner office and began answering phone calls. Many people were seeking my input. I was important and vital, excited about my work and my success.

Suddenly my guided visualization transformed. The sky darkened as the sunshine faded. I felt warm tears streaming down my face. All I could feel was disappointment and sadness. The visualization stopped. The words that remained, repeating over and over in my lingering meditative state were, "If I'm successful, I won't be nice anymore." "If I'm successful, I won't be nice anymore." "If I'm successful, I won't be nice anymore."

At the time of this visualization experience, I hadn't yet learned about the checklist survey. I may have had a different understanding of my experience if I'd been able to recognize that my desire to be a successful professional was in direct conflict with my comprehension of what's required to be an ideal female.

When I shared my visualization with the other women in the group, I was able to experience some humor for and appreciation of my struggle. It has stayed with me all these years, showing how our subconscious can interfere with our truest feelings and our grandest ideals. The socialization brainwashing we aren't even aware of can take control of our perceptions and our choices.

When you experience duality and recognize the ambivalence is out of sync with your core truths, step back and recalculate.

Examine the precepts that are controlling your feelings. Challenge yourself to a new view.

The ideal female and the ideal successful professional person can have limitless versions that work for individual women and that buck the stereotypes and the research. You have to know where the struggle is coming from and understand its main ingredients before you can carve out and live your own version of ideal.

The Impossible Ideal

Keys to Becoming Un-Gagged

- We are often our own barriers to success.

- It's important to understand where our basic beliefs come from.

- It's up to you to define your own ideals.

- Stereotypes are based in common beliefs.

- Recognizing the source of ambivalence can lead to clarity.

The Syndrome of Apology

"I'm sorry you couldn't find the conference room."

"I'm sorry you had to go through such bad traffic."

"I'm sorry I'm the only one who thinks that."

"I'm sorry this is confusing to you."

"I'm sorry you think that's what happened."

"I'm sorry you didn't understand the directions."

"I'm sorry there're things you don't like about this."

"I'm sorry no one has come to take our order."

"I'm sorry you don't like the new proposal."

"I'm sorry."

"I'm sorry."

"I'm sorry."

PUH-LEASE!

STOP WITH THE UNNECESSARY APOLOGIES!

A predominant communication component that needs to be eliminated from female speaking patterns is the apology. Many women habitually insert "I'm sorry" into every situation and conversation. They take responsibility and accept blame for occurrences they have no accountability for and didn't perpetrate. They say they're sorry when there's no requirement for or benefit from blame or apology. This phrase of remorse seems embedded and deeply bound to female self-worth and obligation. Having looked closely at the premises of the Good Girl phenomenon, we can readily understand how the tendency to apologize can arise from good intentions and respectfulness.

Let's acknowledge that respectful communication is desirable. Let's also underscore that apologizing for mistakes or accidental harm is appropriate. Let's finally agree that expressing concern for others' welfare is appreciated and welcome. I would still estimate that more than 90% of the apologies I hear from women are unnecessary and often damaging. It's the frequency, over-use, and disconnected relevance of the apology that causes it to come across badly. Also, frequently repeated phrases will lose their meaning from over-use.

Apology can contribute to lowering your position. When a woman constantly apologizes, she's likely to convey:

- She thinks of herself in a secondary weak way.
- She feels responsible when anything goes wrong.
- She lacks confidence and self-esteem.
- She's afraid she'll be blamed.
- She feels guilty.

Here are some of the opening apologies from this chapter, followed by preferable versions:

AVOID: "I'm sorry you couldn't find the conference room."
BETTER: **"Everyone says our conference room is hard to find. I'll make sure someone meets you in the lobby next time."**

AVOID: "I'm sorry you had to go through such bad traffic."
BETTER: **"We'd be happy to move our meetings to an earlier time to help you avoid the heavy traffic."**

AVOID: "I'm sorry I'm the only one who thinks that."
BETTER: **"I hear how strong everyone's opinions are. I'm happy to listen to others. I have clear beliefs about this."**

AVOID: "I'm sorry this is confusing to you."
BETTER: **"I can hear how confusing this is to you."**

AVOID: "I'm sorry there're things you don't like about this."
BETTER: **"Thanks for telling me what you want changed."**

AVOID: "I'm sorry no one has come to take our order."
BETTER: **"It's taking so long for someone to take our order."**

AVOID: "I'm sorry you don't like the new proposal."
BETTER: **"It sounds like you're dissatisfied with parts of the new proposal."**

Closely aligned with this tendency to over-apologize is the habit many women have of asking permission:

"Is it okay with you if …?"

"Do you mind doing this for me …?"

"I hate to ask you but …?"

"Could I please ask you a question?"

"Will it upset you if I say something about this?"

"Will you do me a favor and let me …?"

"Would it be a problem for me to …?"

"Can I tell you how I see it?"

Being polite is a good thing. Getting someone's buy-in makes sense. Being pushy is a big mistake. Asking permission because you feel intimidated or diminished can be grating. Even worse, it can represent a secondary or childlike demeanor. Adults are peers and equals; they don't need to ask permission before speaking or asking a question.

🔑 Reminder:

Instead of asking for permission, create communications where you are informing people.

Providing information is much better than asking for permission. If you require a green light, use assertive types of introductions to avoid subservience and groveling.

GAGGED

Instead of "begging" or asking if it's okay to speak, start your communications with phrasing similar to these:

"It's important to know you're on board with this."
"Please tell me if you have any objections to ..."
"I have something important to ask you."
"I want to make sure you're informed about ..."
"Here's my view of success. What are your thoughts?"

Apologizing and asking for permission can be a legitimate good communication choice for relevant situations. When used out of habit in uncalled-for circumstances, they reflect submission and inferiority. Save apologies for when you've done something wrong or hurtful. Repeatedly and apologetically asking permission to speak or act, tilts the playing field negatively and diminishes status and professionalism. Stop groveling!

Breaking ingrained habits is easier to recommend than to do. It's challenging to replace the overuse of phrases that have become as involuntary as breathing. Here are tactics you may want to use to adjust unconscious, embedded communication patterns:

Habit Breakers

> ➢ Ask a close friend or family member to snap her fingers each time she hears you say, "I'm sorry."

> ➢ Keep a money jar for a worthy cause nearby and contribute a dollar (or a quarter) each time you ask

permission to speak. (It will work better if you ask someone to monitor this with you.)

➢ Select a few practiced replacement phrases to use to begin your statements: "Thank you for …" "I hear how …" "It's important to tell you …" (Be careful not to replace one communication habit with another.)

Unneeded apologizing and ongoing requests for permission contribute to your not being heard and taken seriously. Adjust these detrimental habits and you'll be on the path to being recognized and respected.

The Syndrome of Apology

Keys to Becoming Un-Gagged

- See yourself on equal footing with others.

- Become aware of and eliminate repetitive speech patterns.

- Look for ways to communicate without subservience.

- Save apologies for when you've done something wrong.

- Communicate as a peer without asking for permission.

⌀ Mechanics of Whining

There are many distinct female voices that come to us through recorded history. I can hear several in my head as vividly as the first time I heard them on television or in a movie. It's intriguing and amusing to take a few female voices from the past and identify what that woman's sound and tone represented, disconnected from the content of her spoken words:

Lucille Ball – whiningly comical and cleverly devious
Mae West – sultry, sexy and invitingly sensual
Maya Angelou – wise, melodic, all-knowing
Minnie Mouse – deferentially mousey and sweetly docile
Tallulah Bankhead – rich, rough and deeply registered

Each voice is a gift. Like a fingerprint, every vocal sound has its own identity. By taking the voice and describing its sound and underlying message without analyzing the spoken words, we can start to understand what the tone, vocal timbre, and resonance might bring to the listener on a subconscious level.

⌨ Reminder:

> *Research tells us that tone of voice is one of the two biggest components of how communication is received.*
> *(The other is facial expression.)*

For years, I've been coaching people on adjusting the attitude they're conveying and the impact they're delivering through their tone of voice. Tone and attitude are wrapped together quite closely.

The underlying contributor to tone of voice and attitude starts with the natural sound of a person's voice. The basic resonance of a woman's voice can have an enormous impact on how she's perceived and on whether and how well she gets heard. The female voice can be the biggest element in how a woman's communication is received and interpreted.

To begin to understand the impact of the sound of the voice, it's worth analyzing and understanding how the human voice evolves. Puberty turns boys to men and girls to women. For a boy, unless he refrains from speaking, his own voice repeatedly announces his arrival into manhood. It's an open public event that cannot be hidden. He now has a man's voice and he's no longer perceived as a boy.

These demarcations set the stage for a man's voice to be heard and for a woman's voice to be of lesser significance. The difference between a girl's voice and her adult voice is minimal. The difference between a boy's voice and his adult voice is night and day.

A striking illustration of this distinct contrast between men's and women's voices is the theatrical device of having a woman play the role of Peter Pan, the boy who won't grow up. It's easy for a woman to sound, look and act like a boy. It's challenging to have a man convincingly sound like a boy, a girl, or a woman, though Dustin Hoffman (Tootsie), Robin Williams (Mrs. Doubtfire), and Eddie Redmayne (The Dutch Girl) all were convincing as women. It would be difficult to envision any of these male actors in the role of a young girl or boy with the voice or body of a child. It's easy to imagine an actress's voice and body transformed believably on stage into a male or female child. These concepts highlight exactly how childlike and secondary a woman's voice and physical aura are perceived to be, in striking contrast to a man's.

We see how women have a few cards stacked against them regarding voice, starting with the deeper tone of a man's voice along with the larger size of his body. The commanding position a man often holds initially comes from his physical size and deepness of voice. When James Earl Jones says, "This is CNN" it's as if he has declared a royal edict wrapped in the deepest purple velvet. When Sam Elliot says, "The Dude abides" (or when Sam Elliot says *anything*) we are carried to somewhere safe, solid, and substantial; we are protected and becalmed, simply from the resonance and buttery inflection of his voice.

When a man becomes angry or agitated, his voice naturally grows deeper and more forceful. When a woman becomes angry or agitated, her voice usually grows higher pitched, more strained, and helplessly, repellingly whinier. It can sound like she's wound up and twisted tightly into a spiral that is screeching to unwind itself.

Even with the vocal and physical imbalance women face, they can still endeavor to capitalize on their demeaner and the vocal elements they can influence and control. Awareness is the first step. Dedication and determination have to follow if the goal is to strengthen and enhance.

How "Soft and Slow" Can "Command and Silence"
As a young, idealistic middle-school French teacher, I had a lot to learn about the internal politics that permeated my New York City

private school. I had a year behind me, teaching in a White Plains public school where my outspoken tendencies were accepted as part of the norm. It took about two weeks into the fall semester for Tia Haye, the Head of the middle school, to pull me aside, tuck me under her wing and explain to me how things worked in this unusual institution owned by an ill-educated banker rather than a scholarly educator. Hierarchy, rather than equality, was the ruling principle there.

After the enlightenment I received from Tia, I became a less outspoken voice in our male-dominated teachers' meetings. I didn't express a word of opposition the day I was required to give up my prep period to cover for another teacher who was out sick. In my prior public school life, substitutes were a matter of course. I kept silent when I had an alternate view from the Head Master or the owner of the school. Tia had given me clear insight into how things worked in this privately owned "financial" institution.

That accepted established hierarchy did not prohibit frequent vociferous power struggles from erupting in our weekly teachers' meetings. I remember men's voices out-blasting each other through escalating turmoil. With the men talking over each other, I was reminded of those chic New York City restaurants where you can barely hear the person facing you. It often felt like we might need to call the security guard to bring back decorum to our meetings.

"That will never work!"
"And I guess you think your idea's better."
"Well, it's definitely better than that crazy concept you just threw on the table for us to consider."
"What backward almanac did you pull that out from?"

"Are you even thinking of what's best for the students?"

It felt out of control and chaotic. Everyone was talking over each other. There was no listening, just shouting.

Then came Tia Haye's soft, controlled, measured, and slow-paced voice. She was speaking almost in a whisper. It felt like you had to stop breathing to avoid drowning out her words. Her eye contact moved from person to person and there were daggers coming from her eyes. She was serious and imposing. Her authority was unquestioned. Her presence was unchallenged. She commanded the room and the chaos ended abruptly as soon as she began to speak.

If anyone had asked me to bet on whether her slow, quiet, measured words would accomplish quiet, consensus, and calm, I would not have placed a wager. Her voice was so quiet that you could barely hear her. And that was the point. With all those men shouting back and forth, she chose the opposite approach. She was dead serious and thereby created dead silence in the room. Everyone was completely hushed. That was the only way to hear her. She was going to say her piece only once. And it was going to be the LAW. Her command of the meeting was immediate and the heated discourse instantly stopped. Quiet attention was achieved.

She didn't repeat or belabor her calmly and firmly stated resolution and no one asked a question. LISTENING was #1. The final decision lay in her hands. When her solution was spoken, that was it. People recognized her firmness and fairness. Her aura was reinforced by her voice. Her voice of firm, quiet authority reigned supreme.

Lessons Learned / Role Models

We can look at Tia Hay's leadership and decision-making skills and give her high marks. It's much more than simply the voice that carried Tia through. To ignore the importance of the voice, especially for women, is to overlook a significantly critical ingredient for paving the way forward.

Just as James Earl Jones and Sam Elliot are examples of the ideal male voice, two women with delicious voices have raised the bar high for female expression and vocal sound:

THE SOUND OF WINNING FEMALE VOICES

Oprah Winfrey – powerfully calm and authoritative, like the smoothness of silk

Allison Janney – firmly grounded and reliable, like a mother's promise that can't be deterred

The more you can download and listen to the sound of such women, the more easily you'll adapt new robust ways to use your voice, to interact with people, and to present yourself effectively.

Use Your Voice to Level the Playing Field

- Breathe deeply from the diaphragm.
- Relax your muscles; avoid tension and tightness.
- Keep your head high.
- Keep your back straight.

- Work on lowering the pitch of your voice.
- Refrain from nasal involvement to avoid sounding like you're whining.
- Avoid escalation of emotion while presenting your position.
- Speak with purpose – not loudly – to command respect.
- Put space around your words to avoid run-on and meandering.
- Use eye contact and facial expression to convey strength.
- Keep anger and frustration out of your voice tone.
- Speak slowly and firmly with conviction.
- Speak up; speak out. (This is about strength of content.)
- Practice; get feedback.
- Practice; get feedback.
- Practice; get feedback.

A professional drama or voice coach can help you achieve a good outcome and can make sure you're incorporating these suggestions safely and correctly.

Without turning ourselves into absurd and impossible renditions of men, we can become aware of and work on many facets of how we're coming across to others, including our breathing patterns, our carriage, and our posture. The goal is to derive from our voices - moderation of tone, depth of character, abundance of self-esteem, and belief in our worth and equality.

✆ Mechanics of Whining

Keys to Becoming Un-Gagged

- Learn to appreciate how multi-layered our voices are.

- Enrich your life by having strong role models.

- Remember how important nonverbal communication is.

- Make developing your voice a high priority.

- Practice deepening your voice's pitch to eliminate whining.

✍ Forgetting to Listen

It feels like no one talks to anyone anymore. Texting, email, and social media have become the principal methods of communication. There's less direct spoken communication than ever before. People get out of the habit of listening because they're responding to or creating written communications most of the time. Given our current climate, it's questionable if it makes sense to include a chapter on "*Listening*" in this book.

Asking that question actually recognizes and reinforces the increased need for an examination of this topic. Today's circumstances demand it. If we stop placing a value on listening, we then become isolated and doomed; we might as well stop communicating altogether.

"Forgetting to Listen" is a pervasive occurrence disconnected from gender. Rather than dissect and declare the specific amount of neglected listening attributed to males vs. females, I'd rather present the nuances I often see in women's typical communication and listening patterns.

Women often express empathy more easily than men and think of empathy as a valued human characteristic. If we look at the key elements of Emotional Intelligence laid out by Daniel Goleman, we'll see the essential value of empathy underscored as a desirable primary soft skill, strongly related to beneficial interpersonal dynamics and business success.

It's a challenge as a coach to make sure I support the feelings of the individual I'm coaching as well as help that person express what she's experiencing. It can feel like a betrayal to my gender to recommend that a woman benefits from avoiding touchy-feely words so that she can be taken seriously. This advice goes back to our earlier review of the adjectives people check to describe ideal successful individuals.

One of the traps of emotional language is that sympathetic communications and supportive outpourings can be categorized as maternal or overly feminine. There's nothing inherently wrong with being maternal and showing empathy. They are positive traits. If we refer to the adjective checklist survey (in *The Impossible Ideal* chapter), we can easily understand how rarely (if at all) adjectives like "empathetic" are checked for the ideal male and for the ideal successful person. The goal is to respect the qualities that are important to you and to who you are without over-exposing or over-emphasizing emotional language. Empathy falls into the "keeper" category; it's an esteemed attribute. Being empathetic – understanding where people are coming from and what they might be experiencing – is a prized, essential asset.

While empathy can be a significant contributor to good listening, empathy can also fall short of the genuine reinforcement and engagement that comes with focused, validated listening. Even when empathy is the main event in an exchange, real listening may fall by the wayside. Women often forget to listen even while they're being extremely empathetic. Empathizing and listening require different focal points.

You can be attentively empathetic without attentively listening.

When a woman empathizes, she might say something like, "Oh, you poor thing." and then quickly revert to her standby apology: "I'm so sorry you're having such a hard time getting your report finished in time for our meeting."

Another type of emblematic response a woman might declare is, "That's really awful. I hate it when I have to deal with that kind of painful situation. You never know how upsetting these things can be for everyone."

In both examples, the empathy is genuine. The communication is full of emotions yet the validated listening is weak. The emphasis is on the speaker's feelings and the emotional challenges of the other person rather than on the specifics of the dilemma the individual is facing.

Reminder:

There's a way to express care and support for others genuinely without coating the communication in emotions.
There's great advantage for women to express viewpoints and observations without wrapping them in emotional language.

It's easy to replace emotional word choices with neutral or rational words without diminishing the intent or value of the communication. Doing so increases the strength and relevance of what you're saying, augmenting your ability to be heard and taken seriously.

> Replace "I feel" with "I think" or "I see"

> Instead of saying "People will be very upset." say, "This will have a big impact on the group."

> Rather than describe a situation this way, "I hate how long it takes to ..." say, "It would be better if we could shorten the process by ..."

🗝 Reminder:

An important key to good workplace communication and to a woman's being heard, respected and appreciated, is through validated listening, expressed in rational unemotional language.

Validating what a person has just said, demonstrates you're listening. When a person genuinely hears, through the words of the listener, that his or her situation has been taken in and understood, the communication can enhance business endeavors, establish strong relationships, and decrease conflict and disagreement.

Validating what a person has just said is different from agreeing with that person. The focus is on showing how well you heard what was communicated.

Let's look at the language of validated listening and how it goes beyond empathetic listening (also paying attention to the deletion of emotional language):

AVOID: "Oh, you poor thing. I'm so sorry you're having such a hard time getting your report finished in time for our meeting."

BETTER: "You've put a lot of time and dedicated work into this. I hear what a challenge it is to get the calculations completed and folded into the report in time for our 4:00 meeting."

AVOID: "That's really awful. I hate it when I have to deal with that kind of painful situation. You never know how upsetting these things can be for everyone."

BETTER: "Thank you for keeping me informed about the situation. I appreciate knowing how you see what you're up against. Let's stay in touch so we can monitor if there's any further escalation that requires immediate attention."

AVOID: "I feel so bad for you. You must be angry that you have to deal with this when it wasn't your fault it got dumped in your lap at the last minute."

BETTER: "I can see this took you completely by surprise. It's difficult to set priorities when facing unexpected events like these. I can ask if one of my team members can work with you to help you get this resolved quickly."

> **Reminder:**
>
> *Listening requires engagement.*
>
> *Listening is reflected by validation.*
>
> *Validation is different from agreement.*

In these recommended types of responses, the empathy remains strong and the demonstration of validated listening reveals detailed attention.

The Good Girl tendency is also likely to come into play in the *listening* aspects of a woman's work life. Her thinking and the myths she believes may unfold like this:

Encircled by Myth

If I'm a good girl, I follow the rules. If I follow the rules, I expect others to do the same. If I see following the rules as black and white, I may stop listening to others' extraneous views because the rules are clear. If I see the rules as clear, I can think there's only one way to accomplish a goal. If I think there's only one way to do something, I'll lose sight of the fact that there're always many ways to achieve most goals. If I lose sight of multiple options, I'll stop listening to others.

If I stop listening to others, I'll miss nuance after nuance and likely stop people from being independent. If I stop people from being independent, I'll become someone who is out of tune and out of step with those around me. If I become out of tune and out of step with those around me, I probably won't even see my own contribution to how I arrived at such a disconnected place where I am forgetting to listen.

A woman's focus on solutions and doing the right thing can inadvertently carve out a narrow path. Creating limitations rather than widening options and accepting different innovative approaches can result in people closing down and turning off.

Receptivity to a variety of viewpoints, listening attentively to others, keeping people in the loop, welcoming input from co-workers, paying attention to the comments of many, validating an array of perspectives, all pave the way to being recognized and appreciated as a good listener and an equitable leader.

Forgetting to Listen

Keys to Becoming Un-Gagged

- Empathy provides a foundation for Emotional Intelligence.

- Email, texting and social media are diluting communications.

- Women benefit from avoiding flowery emotional language.

- Listening to and validating others enhances communication.

- It's essential to challenge the myths we secretly tell ourselves.

Conscientiousness to the Extreme

Conscientiousness goes hand in glove with having a strong moral compass and a high-level work ethic. These are characteristics that contribute positively to every workplace. Can you have too much of a good thing? Does conscientiousness have an underbelly?

Female Identity

The road to conscientiousness is linked to female identity starting at an early age. The little girl models herself after her mother or the primary female authority figures in her life. The little girl wants to do the *Right Thing* and be the *Good Girl*.

Most girls uphold the family values and the practices of the female family members they look up to. I can remember as a tiny child visiting someone's home and seeing the available first sheet of toilet paper in the bathroom hanging from the top of the roll facing towards me. I knew that was *wrong* and wanted to *fix* it. In our home, we placed the roll in the holder with the new sheet coming out from the back and bottom of the roll.

It feels odd to remember that so vividly since I was quite young. I didn't see it as a different choice from the preferred choice in my home; I saw it as a *mistake* that other families were making. I think I experienced this reaction before I even knew how to take the roll from the holder and reverse its installation. I imagine that once I was a little older and had learned how to do that, I probably inappropriately exchanged the position of the toilet paper in other people's homes. That's the kind of "conscientiousness" I grew up experiencing. There was a clear distinction between the right and wrong way to do everything. I was dedicated to carrying out corrections and adhering to a certain prescriptive path.

With an older sister who rarely chose avenues that pleased our parents, I was determined to do everything right. The consequences for making the wrong choices, even at such a young age, felt huge: the withdrawal of love and the loss of self-definition. Identity became closely tied to doing everything correctly and to pleasing others.

Today, of course, I would never want to impose any of my preferences on others or judge anyone for a toilet paper roll placement. There's no circumstance where I would see it as appropriate to rearrange objects in someone's home. Ironically, in my home currently, I've come to prefer the toilet paper installed with the paper coming from the top of the roll – the opposite of my childhood requirement.

What an odd example to demonstrate early dedication to conscientiousness. It vividly demonstrates growing up with clear ways to do the Right Thing and be the Good Girl. It also represents how identity forms.

The carry-over of conscientiousness - and its connection to female identity - into the world of work, can weigh heavily for many women:

> - Most women go beyond the minimum requirements.
> - Most women don't cut corners or look for shortcuts.
> - Most women avoid cover-up and exaggeration.

- Most women rarely refuse requests.
- Most women want to help.
- Most women place importance on building relationships.

Paradox Revealed

You would think these traits would make it hard to label conscientiousness as one of the mistakes that keep women from being heard at work. You would think these attributes would naturally contribute to a woman being respected and appreciated. Instead, these characteristics can contribute to women being taken for granted and being seen as secondary worker-bees rather than proactive innovative leaders.

A theme can emerge from conscientiousness that is similar to *The Good Girl and the Cookie* syndrome we looked at earlier. Sometimes a conscientious woman fades to the background, working diligently, waiting for reward and recognition. It's easy to take advantage of the conscientious worker-bee without rewarding or recognizing her.

⚷ Reminder:

> *Conscientiousness can be a passive attribute that diminishes initiative.*

These excellent work habits can lead to burnout. Even good traits like conscientiousness, when carried to extreme, can be damaging. Anything that is over-used will break.

Getting lost in conscientiousness provides a smokescreen for avoiding networking and professional development. It's easy to rationalize how you don't have time for external events and meetings or the ability to take a vacation or socialize with friends, since you're up to your eyeballs in the demands and requirements of your work. These always sound like legitimate reasons:

> "I can't make any plans to go to lunch with you this week. I have to get my office re-organized and looking more professional before our CEO arrives on Friday."

> "I've been wanting to attend the ABCD monthly meetings since I joined in January. There's always something extra I have to take care of that keeps me from leaving work early enough to get there before the meeting is over."

> "I have to stay late tonight to do some more research for the upcoming pitch to XYZ Corp at the end of the month. No matter how much I prepare, there's always some crazy question that catches me off guard."

> "I keep meaning to call Barbara to make a plan with her. There're just too many demands on me right now and she keeps slipping to the bottom of my want-to-do list."

It's important to realize that when you use this kind of language, there're usually other elements underneath. You might be avoiding facing other realities. You might be making excuses to cover up your lack of willingness or desire to make changes. You might be afraid of your ability to get the outcomes you desire.

🗝 Reminder:

> **Avoid using phrases like**
> **"I can't" "I have to" "There's no way I can"**
> **Avoid passive victimized language.**

It's difficult to know when your work ethic and moral compass have blocked out your reality barometer. It's easy to get trapped behind the demands of your home life and workload rather than make the time and take the steps to invest in your personal development and life enrichment. Women struggle with this in their family roles and as workers. The duality factor we've looked at can often double down! (Hmmmm, does that make it the quadruple factor? ...)

Questions for Keeping the Balance

Here's a set of key questions to ask yourself. Raw honesty and a good long look in the mirror will be required to answer them well. I recommend purchasing a special journal and writing out these thoughtful responses by hand to keep, expand and regularly review:

➢ What are your top 10 values? What 10 qualities, entities, or endeavors do you value most? Define each of them with your own personal definition. Place them in order of importance from 1-10 (#1= most important) to you personally (not to the world).

➢ If there were no financial limitations or family responsibility impediments in your life, what would your life look like?

➢ How would you spend the money if you won the mega millions lottery and it was required that you could only spend the money on yourself?

➢ How would you spend the money if you won the mega millions lottery and it was required that you spend the money on anyone and anything except yourself?

➢ For what accomplishments, would you like to receive a lifetime achievement award near the end of your life? If you were writing the speech to honor you for this award, what would that speech say?

> How did answering these questions change your perceptions or goals? How did answering these questions change you?

A good leader is comfortable rolling up her sleeves and working side by side with her team. At the same time, a good leader must set herself apart to make big decisions, to keep people on track, to meet larger objectives, and to provide direction. It's up to you to make sure you don't become hidden in conscientious productivity, while neglecting career and personal development activities that will help you advance your career, bring advantages to your employer, and most of all contribute to balanced, thriving, mental and physical health.

Small Steps to Bring Balance to Conscientiousness

> Make a list of mini (non-caloric, non-alcoholic) activities you love; do at least one/up to three every day. (Examples: mini crossword puzzle, 5-minute meditation, bubble bath, knitting, journal writing, take a walk outside, tend plants, read for pleasure, call a friend)

> Create a time limit system at work and at home that gives you a variety of involvement in different tasks.

> Make a commitment to meet deadlines with intermittent rewards and breaks along the way.

➢ If you're extraverted, save the socializing for after you've met a certain milestone. If you're an introvert, commit to socializing before tackling a solitary isolated activity.

➢ Make plans with friends/a friend and meet regularly. (restaurant, gym, movie, concert, theater, park)

Conscientiousness matters. It's connected to your core values and standards that no one can take from you. The key is looking for balance; the key is making balance happen; the key is holding on to balance.

🔑 **Reminder:**

The antidote for duality is balance.

Conscientiousness to the Extreme

Keys to Becoming Un-Gagged

- Monitor the demands you put on yourself to avoid burnout.

- Remember the importance of demonstrating initiative.

- Be the one who speaks up for what's important to you.

- Make sure people are aware of your dedication.

- Bring balance and responsibility to career management.

✍ The Imposition of Standards

Having guiding principles to light your path will give you direction and strengthen your journey. Standards are valuable when they help you stay focused. Benchmarks can be highly beneficial when they're clearly defined and shared, inspiring and motivating people to achieve mutual goals.

We've looked at the significance of standards a few times in preceding chapters. What we still need to see is what happens when standards are imposed rather than inspired.

There are two pitfalls where a woman's standards can lead to trouble, turning benefits to damage:

Pitfall #1: Imposing her personal standards on others without their desire, understanding, or buy-in.

Pitfall #2: Feeling like she'll be judged badly because of the lack of standards or different standards of the people surrounding her.

The perfect storm will come as no surprise, following the premises of The Good Girl and the Cookie, The Impossible Ideal, The Syndrome of Apology, Mechanics of Whining, Forgetting to Listen, and Conscientiousness to the Extreme. It's only natural that the resulting, finely-tuned, brilliantly shining standards will become so deeply entrenched that they'll no longer be conscious voluntary selections and instead will become as compulsory as breathing.

The over-achieving woman may be so attached to her standards that she can think they're embedded the same way in everyone else. When she becomes a leader, her rigid adherence to the rules and to her absolute code of ethics can entrap her and spill over to everyone around her. It's like part of her DNA. She has honed every move along the way and each step must be exactly right. Each must be measured, reviewed and verified. The years of conscientiousness can easily turn into micro-managing, judgment and whip-cracking.

Since she's raised the bar so high, she's sure that everyone else sees the same standards as she does. She's stunned when her 360 feedback reveals that her team thinks she's breathing down their necks. They feel like she's always ready to pounce. They report they cannot do their jobs well because she's always making them go back and do things the way she always did them when she was in their roles. The problem is there's often much more advanced technology and better methods that have been incorporated since she was in their jobs. Mimicking her methods may duplicate efforts, consume much more time than required, and replicate data that's already analyzed and stored.

Her tendency is to dig in: that's the way she always did it or that's the way *she* sees as the best way to do it now, so that's what she's demanding of her team. The standards are shining bright and there's no way she can tolerate abandoning them or cutting corners. It's like an uncontrollable obsession. She finds herself re-doing and duplicating a great deal of her team's work because when she doesn't review each purchase order, merchandise update, and branch transaction, she can't sleep at night. She feels like Don Quixote attacking the windmill. She sees herself as the woman of exacting standards leading the charge.

I've been asked to estimate the percentage of women executives I've coached who fit the preceding description. I would estimate it's more than 75%. The irony is that these women have the highest standards imaginable and are dedicated managers who are committed to doing what's best for employees, employers and themselves. They're looking at what brought them to the successful point where they are in their careers and want, more than anything, for others to be successful too. They're committed to their standards and want others to follow in their footsteps.

Here's the most blatant example I've witnessed of The Imposition of Standards, where a woman's dedication to principles went too far:

Thomas's Office

Whenever Sharon, the Senior Vice President of Corporate Affairs, came to Atlanta from the company headquarters in Philly to troubleshoot her team's current issues and help put out fires, everyone knew work would come to a standstill as they responded to her inquisitions and demands. They all knew that Sharon would keep them from getting their high-priority work accomplished. Of course, she always chose to visit at the end of the month when the pressures were the highest and when the team needed to be free from preparing extraneous reports, being drilled on obscure future events, and spending wasted time in irrelevant meetings with Sharon.

On one of her visits at crunch time, Sharon decided Atlanta's Managing Director, Thomas, needed to address the chaos and disorder in his office. Sharon thought he couldn't possibly be doing high-quality work or leading well when his office looked like a tornado had just swept through. She wanted him to be the perfect role model, just like she was. She was going to be the knight in shining armor and do something about the mess. It was unprofessional. Thomas's office looked disgraceful.

In the middle of the day, at the height of client and staff traffic moving past Thomas's open doorway, with the blinds raised on the glass partition wall separating Thomas's office from the main conference room, Sharon set herself up in his office with three big empty filing boxes, a dolly for carting the boxes away, and a giant shredder from the supply room.

When Thomas came back to his office from a meeting with the market analysts, Sharon was waiting there to ambush him. Before he could take off his jacket or check his email, Sharon was ordering him around his own office. She'd already removed the file folders he had lining the window sills and stacked them on the floor in the separate piles she'd designated as significant. Thomas was crushed with anger, panic and embarrassment. Everyone could see what was happening. Everyone knew what a micro-manager Sharon was. Everyone had tremendous sympathy for Thomas. No one was surprised that Sharon would go that far; yet, it was a most shocking event to witness. Poor Thomas now had no way to locate folders or signed contracts that were easily at his fingertips less than an hour earlier.

Sharon was Thomas's immediate superior. He respected her business acumen and dedication. He was a straight shooter who esteemed hierarchy and never complained about his superiors. Thomas would never throw anyone under the bus. He saw how particular Sharon was. He knew his chaotic methodologies were foreign and upsetting to her. He knew that, because of his unique "organizing" system, if anything happened to him, no one else would be able to locate required materials or documents. Thomas knew he needed to bring more order to his personal methods of managing administrative details. Sharon had told Thomas to get rid of the clutter and chaos for many months.

There were certainly legitimate perspectives on both sides of this story. There was zero legitimacy, though, to support the public display of Sharon taking over Thomas's office, physically dismantling and re-ordering his "filing" system, and ordering him around as if he were a four-year-old who'd pulled every toy in his room off the shelves and then dismantled the furniture that was holding them. My son did that years ago, and even then, I actually laughed at the sight, took several photos to commemorate the mess, and then **calmly discussed and oversaw the steps he was going to take** to change chaos back to order in his room.

This extreme, cautionary tale also represents the second pitfall mentioned earlier. The real driver behind this story is Sharon's concern that Thomas's messy office would reflect badly on her. This rigid imposition of standards is often accompanied by fear of exposure as a failure. If she couldn't get anything done in the middle of chaos, it must follow that people would see Thomas's disarray as a reflection of Sharon's dysfunction. He worked for her, so his disorder diminished how people saw her. Sharon couldn't separate those two ideas and experienced them as one.

Her conscientiousness and dedication carried over to everything. She was on her way to overload and burnout. She was demotivating the people she most wanted to inspire to do their jobs effectively and successfully.

Sharon needed to learn how to ask meaningful questions and have conversations that would lead people to develop their own methods to reach the team goals. When she stifled the initiatives of her team, they may have been doing what she wanted them to do but their actions were robotic and mechanical. They couldn't absorb the foundation of reason and value for their choices and would eventually return to their own devices, the way they'd always done. They may have even resentfully rejected her preferred methods because she had forced them on people and so they'd ended up sabotaging purposefully or unconsciously. Either way, the result was less than optimum.

Here are the kind of questions Sharon, and other women leaders like Sharon, can start asking people to begin balanced conversations that bring out authentic development, genuine dedication, and natural un-imposed standards:

- How would you describe what's most important to you about your job?
- What motivates you the most to do your job well?
- What are your proudest professional accomplishments?
- How did you choose your career?
- What's been the biggest influence in your life?

Open thoughtful discussions that naturally flow from questions like these are the key to getting people's buy-in and commitment to the standards that are most beneficial at work.

More specifically, here are some talking points that Sharon could have introduced to avoid the damaging showdown with Thomas:

- I'd like to talk with you about your office.
- Tell me about how you organize your workflow.
- What do you see as the impact of your office on others?
- What benefits or disadvantages would come from your office being more orderly?
- What enhancements can you comfortably agree to that would bring more order to your office?

These questions invite discussion and open the door for listening. Notice that the question "Why" is purposefully missing from the suggestions. "Why" can sound accusatory and it's best to use other open-ended approaches. Using a level tone of voice will help in avoiding intimidation, judgment, and accusation.

Here is a significant story to finalize this meaningful chapter on standards, on what they mean to people, on how they influence the choices people make, and on the degree of excellence they produce:

Building Mandela's Red Mercedes

When Nelson Mandela was released from prison after 27 years, the workers in the East London, South Africa Mercedes manufacturing plant asked to hand-make a red S-Class Mercedes for Mandela, to pay tribute to his dedicated sacrifice and to celebrate the end of apartheid. The executives of the company agreed to their goal and provided the parts without requiring payment. The car was made by many workers as a symbol of the years of imprisonment and struggle through apartheid horrors that had existed in South Africa for so long.

The workers asked to do this during unpaid overtime; they worked one hour extra at the end of each workday to accomplish their goal. Footage covering their work shows them dancing and singing in celebration as they worked. All the Mercedes workers wanted to be a part of the project; they wanted to make sure their hands contributed to building Mandela's red Mercedes. The color red was selected to represent the bloodshed during all those years of apartheid reign.

Prior Mercedes automobiles that were built in the same plant by the same workers consistently had numerous manufacturing errors. Yet when Mandela's red Mercedes was made by hand, those same workers produced an automobile that was flawless. There were no errors in the manufacture of Mandela's Mercedes.

The standards of building a Mercedes had existed from the beginning of Mercedes Benz as a company. The pride of manufacturing in Germany and other Mercedes manufacturing plants superseded and coincided with those that existed or were barely embraced in South Africa prior to the end of apartheid and the building of Mandela's red Mercedes S-Class.

It's a magnificent reflection to see how the standards changed organically and spontaneously when the workers knew that the car they were building was for Nelson Mandela. When standards are naturally defined and personally claimed, the outcomes will be greatly enhanced. When standards are imposed or forced without dedication or buy-in, the outcomes will be inferior and unreliable.

8 The Imposition of Standards:

Keys to Becoming Un-Gagged

⊷ Avoid thinking you can impose your standards on others.

⊷ Make it a goal to inspire people to embrace a strong work ethic.

⊷ Be the best role model you can be.

⊷ Ask open-ended questions to encourage meaningful dialog.

⊷ Know that people see you differently from your self-image.

✂ The Vicious Cycle:
Feedback, Guilt and Defensiveness

In my book *SPEAK EASY, The Communication Guide for Career and Life Success*, I emphasize the value of feedback. It's impossible to know the impact we're having without feedback from those around us. We're often so intent on what we think we've expressed and what we wanted to convey that we remain mostly unaware of how our communication has been experienced and interpreted.

Research has shown that 93% of how communication is received comes from the nonverbal, having nothing to do with the words. Tone of voice and facial expression have the biggest impact on how people interpret and experience what others say to them.

How Communication Is Received

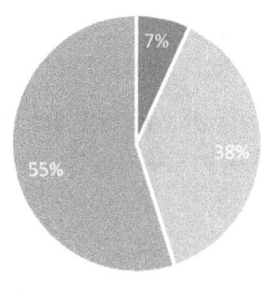

■ Verbal　■ Voice　■ Body Language

Being open to feedback and making sure it's part of our everyday experience are essential for self-awareness and self-development. It's often difficult for women to hear others' views about them without experiencing their input as criticism. Since only 7% of how people receive communication comes from the words, it's easy to lose track of the content and become lost in the reactions that are coming from the 93% of communication interpretation that naturally occurs.

🗝 Reminder:

> ***Train yourself to hear and experience what's being said as <u>information</u> only.***
>
> ***<u>Learn</u> from feedback rather than <u>feel</u> from feedback.***

Adhering to this advice to disconnect feelings from feedback is complex. Since we've examined The Imposition of Standards and also recognize how females create a high bar for their achievement, it's easy to see how quickly they start to feel guilty in response to feedback they've heard as criticism. Let's look at a definition of the word 'guilt' to see more clearly how it can sabotage the benefits of receiving feedback:

🗝 Definition:

> **GUILT: *A feeling of remorse or responsibility for a transgression, crime, or wrong-doing either real or imagined***

When a woman experiences guilt in response to feedback, two outcomes are likely to occur:

1. The valuable content and potential learning opportunity are obliterated.
2. The natural tendency to disprove the criticism turns into embedded defensiveness, likely to inhibit growth.

It's critical for women to break the cycle of feedback, guilt, and defensiveness to gain the fullest value possible from those who are observing their strengths and weaknesses and providing them with diverse perspectives.

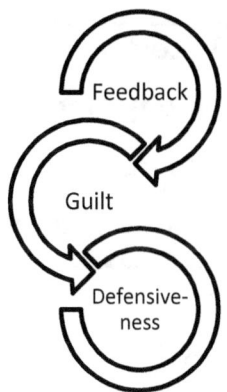

It can be highly challenging for the dedicated conscientious woman to receive feedback without experiencing guilt and defensiveness. I see the roots for feeling guilty coming from an even deeper level than the Wonder Woman's vigilant exhausting goal of wanting to save the day and do everything right. I see a woman's guilt as a cry for love. It's decidedly painful for a woman to endeavor to do everything "The Right Way" and still feel, through her interpretation of feedback, that she isn't liked. Equating feedback with whether she's liked can be the #1 Achilles Heel a woman in the workplace experiences. It can feel like the annihilation of her identity. It's why the tears ran down my cheeks in the guided visualization where I fell apart because if I became successful, I wouldn't be likeable anymore.

Having strong relationships in the workplace will always be an asset. Getting along well with people is also highly valuable.

Popularity cannot be the main driver for a good leader. Wanting to be liked as a major priority is likely to result in unwanted and destructive outcomes.

🗝 Quote:

> *"If you set out to be liked, you would be prepared to compromise on anything at any time and you would achieve nothing."*
> **Margaret Thatcher, Former Prime Minister of Britain**

There's no such thing as inaccurate or incorrect feedback. Feedback reflects how people are experiencing what you're doing and saying. The impact others say you're having on them is always correct, no matter how far it is from your intention.

Here are recommended ways to respond to feedback that feels hurtful or that you experience as criticism. These types of responses can alleviate feelings of guilt, build your receptivity to feedback, and encourage others to continue to be open and forthcoming.

Feedback Responses:

- "It's important to know how you view what happened."
- "Thanks for being honest and sharing your views."
- "I hope you'll continue to express your opinions so I can know where you're coming from on this."

> "What further details can you add so I'll fully understand?"

Here's a series of suggested questions you can routinely ask yourself and others to establish a method of getting regular feedback:

Feedback Questions:
1. What are my strengths?
2. What am I doing well?
3. What are my areas for development?
4. What do I need to do differently?
5. What are my blind spots? What's missing from my radar screen?***
6. What's the best advice you would give me?
7. What's missing from these questions that's important?

(*** #5 is a question only others can answer. If you have an answer for it, it's not a blind spot.)

Comparing your answers to those you get from others can help you identify how closely aligned your interactions are with your intentions and goals.

Out of feedback comes the opportunity to create a development plan for your future. Establishing a plan for how you want to incorporate valuable feedback into self-enhancement will contribute to your professional development and maximize the benefit of receiving feedback. Working with a coach or mentor can also be essential to gaining lasting benefit from valuable feedback.

To receive the Top Ten Tips for Receiving Feedback and the Top Ten Tips for Giving Feedback, go to:
TodaysEmpoweredWoman.com/Be-Heard

To receive a detailed step by step Development Plan template, incorporating your strengths and development areas, go to:
TodaysEmpoweredWoman.com/Be-Heard

The Vicious Cycle:
Feedback, Guilt and Defensiveness

Keys to Becoming Un-Gagged

- Our impact may be different from our intent.

- Guilt is a destructive overlay to productive process and action.

- Defensiveness is a barrier to growth and learning.

- A development plan is an excellent way to maximize feedback.

- It's valuable to make feedback an integral part of your life.

✺ Attachment to the Personal

In the preceding chapters, we've seen some obvious connections between a woman's principles and her tendency to take things personally. Women are often accused of being too emotional. They are frequently admonished, especially at work, for experiencing everything personally.

Let's look at each prior chapter and identify the typical thread in the female tapestry that contributes to these labels of being too emotional and taking things too personally.

➢ **The Good Girl and the Cookie**:

"If they really liked me, they'd give me a cookie."

➢ **The Impossible Ideal**:

"If I become too successful, they won't like me anymore."

➢ **The Syndrome of Apology**:

"I'm sorry they didn't like me enough to include me in their planning meeting."

➢ **Mechanics of Whining**:

"I guess if they'd liked the sound of my voice, they'd have invited me to go with them."

- ➢ **Forgetting to Listen:**

    "If I'd listened more carefully and validated their ideas better, they might have thought I was smart enough to join their group."

- ➢ **Conscientiousness to the Extreme:**

    "If I don't do the right thing, they'll think I don't care."

- ➢ **The Imposition of Standards:**

    "If I don't do the right thing, they'll think I'm unethical."

- ➢ **The Vicious Cycle: Feedback, Guilt and Defensiveness:**

    "If I don't do the right thing, they'll think I'm lazy."

The one instructive element that cries out from these synthesized female statements, is the concern women have about what others think of them. If you're taking what's happening personally and you're choosing responses and actions based on what you suspect others think of you, that's a slippery slope, quite hard to climb back up the hill from.

When I asked women to talk with me about how they see this topic – Attachment to the Personal – and how important they think it is as one of The 10 Mistakes That Stop Women From Being Heard At Work, these are some of their responses:

"This is my biggest issue at work."

"This is the most important factor in my productivity."

"This has a significant impact on my sense of self-worth."

"This has been the biggest stumbling block in my career."

"This is the most important topic for women at work."

"This is what keeps me up at night and robs my creativity."

"This is the thing that most separates men from women."

Clearly, it's important to examine this topic lovingly and with care. In thinking about the facets we've looked at up till now:

>apology
>
>conscientiousness
>
>defensiveness
>
>feedback
>
>guilt
>
>listening
>
>permission
>
>standards

the one underlying commonality is the connective tissue. In the search for female identity and accomplishment, there's almost always a tie back to the "other."

🔑 Reminder:

> ***Women are about connection.***

While most men are driven by "winning," most women (who may also like winning) set priorities based on:

- how accurately others understand them
- how well they're meeting others' demands
- how well they're meeting others' expectations
- how what they're doing impacts others
- if others approve of them
- if others care about them
- if others like them
- if they are appreciated
- will someone hurt their feelings
- will they be loved
- will they hurt someone's feelings
- will what they're doing cause others to suffer
- will what they're doing help others

That's a pretty big list to be carrying around and worrying about all the time. It reminds me of a homeless woman I saw near Fifth Avenue one night:

The Shopping Bag Lady

Wearing three layers of ragged clothing under her coat, she had two overflowing shopping carts, three full, tattered shopping bags and a huge rolling suitcase. She was slowly heading west on 54th Street and could only move two of her carrier items at a time. After making one drop-off, she would go back to gather more of her stuff and had to repeat that lugging act about four times before starting anew with the original load. Obviously, she was making slow headway.

What she needed, to be able to get anywhere, was to edit her belongings down to one large backpack she could attach behind her shoulders and successfully make her way forward.

My thinking about how to improve her mobility did nothing to change her challenges that night but her image became indelibly burned in my memory.

She became a haunting inspiration for when I'm feeling overloaded and stuck. Frequently, as I coach women getting in touch with what's bogging them down and holding them back, we whittle away to lessen the load they're carrying so that it will feel like it fits in a backpack that won't weigh or slow them down.

The ideals many women espouse, the responsibilities they carry, the depth of emotions they feel, the history they've experienced, and their attachment to the personal contribute to their most treasured assets and best endeavors. There's a fine line that, when crossed, turns those feelings and baggage into the overload of our shopping bag lady. We can recognize we've stepped over that line when our feelings are far out of proportion to the current circumstances, when our emotions feel out of our control, and when we seem to have no way of stopping the flow. It can be embarrassing and frightening when our feelings seem to be in control of us rather than our being in control of them. It feels like a child has snuck inside us and taken over. And that's exactly what's happening.

Here's an excerpt from *SPEAK EASY, The Communication Guide for Career and Life Success* to shine a light on how to achieve the balancing act required to lovingly manage the child within and take charge of our attachment to the personal:

~~~~~~~~~~~~~~~~~~~~~~~~~~~~~

The Child Within

When we experience extreme emotional reactions to what people are saying, there's usually something from our personal history that is stimulating those emotions. Whenever our feelings are out of proportion to an actual situation and we feel that our feelings and responses are out of control, there's often an underlying link to our past.

Our usual response to these out of control feelings is to reprimand ourselves for the childish demeaning behavior. This self-admonition and strong negative emotional response reflects a disconnection from our life history and a rejection of the child from our past who lives inside each of us. It's certainly better to focus on and be in the present than to live in and dwell on the past, yet if we never come to terms with, understand, and embrace the child who lives inside each of us, then it will remain difficult to live fully in the present and our emotions will control us rather than our being able to control our emotions.

As foreign as the concept of the child within may seem or as much as it sounds like touchy-feely psychobabble, it's a predominant obstacle many people face and you may be one of them. Without recognition, self-acceptance and true self-affection, the child within will continue to dominate your feelings and control how you see the world, how you react to it and how you communicate.

The time and work it takes to arrive at a new place of self-acceptance requires dedication and often the benefit of professional support. There's certainly an abundance of literature that focuses in depth on these elements connected to the inner child. Rather than cite them or go into detail on this important topic that greatly influences how we function, here are some brief guidelines to begin to incorporate a new understanding of and a gentler approach to the child within:

- *Examine the situations when you have exaggerated feelings or emotions/communications that are out of control.*
- *Look back at these situations to see if you can find the reprimanding judgmental self-talk going on in your head.*
- *Establish, as best as you can, what age in your childhood or youth you think these reprimands most typically stem from.*
- *Think of the loving age-appropriate ways you can be self-accepting and loving towards that child.*
- *Develop a set of embracing new language to express to your child within.*
- *Find warmth and humor to engage the child rather than impatience and rejection.*
- *Be self-loving.*

With sensitivity to the setting and the individual, when I see people dealing with repeating life-obstacles, I selectively examine with them what connection there is between the reoccurring obstacles and the child within.

~~~~~~~~~~~~~~~~~~~~~~~~~~~

Here is an Inner Child experience to provide more insight into a subject that's often hard to wrap your brain around:

The Three-Year-Old

My two closest friends and fellow students in the Masters in Counseling program both were enthusiastically into the Inner Child dynamic. I listened to their dedicated preaching and espousing of this Inner Child approach to emotional issues; I just didn't buy into it the way they did. I had determined that my inner child was about three years old. She seemed happy and undemanding and I couldn't quite see what she had to do with any of my emotional responses and borderline depression, as a 34-year-old mother going through a divorce.

She was such a good girl and, for sure, was the favorite daughter. She repeatedly and confidently said to everyone, "You love me, don't-cha?" "Adorable!" everyone said.

Really, I'd tried to get into praising her affectionately, but come on! She wasn't actually around anymore and I had my son and myself to be concerned about.

One morning I was getting ready for work and was putting on make-up. The wall facing me was covered in mirror and, not unlike other mornings, tears started to run down my cheeks while I was putting on mascara. Definitely not a good combination. The more I thought about my messed-up existence, how I'd contributed to the end of my marriage, and how I no longer was surrounded by an elegant, respected lifestyle and mate, the harder the tears fell and the more out of control I felt.

Somehow, I found myself staring into the mirror, looking deeply into the eyes of the three-year-old. The tears stopped immediately, the moment I looked at her lovingly and said calmly, strongly, and with true affection, "I know you're hurting. I know you're scared. I love you and I'm going to take care of you. I get how terrified you are. You have to stop doing this. You can't barge in and disrupt everything like this anymore. You can't. I won't abandon you. I'm right here by your side all the time. Enough is enough. I won't let you do this anymore.".

Everything changed in that moment. I could feel her fear evaporating. She felt safe and protected. She looked right back at me and said,

"Thank you. Why didn't you stop me before?"

The next time I met my grad school girlfriends for coffee, I was the one testifying about the Inner Child. That experience brought me a new life. I certainly have cried since that day in the mirror and have had emotional responses to what's happening in my life. I have never again had an unexplainable, out-of-control, disproportionate meltdown since then. I'm grateful to my fellow students and appreciative of the balance I gained.

The goal is to find the way forward while traveling much lighter.

⊷ Reminder:

> **There is no baggage-free ride in life.**

We all get scars and gain our unique histories. When we can reach inside, appreciate our past, and accept where the out of control feelings are coming from, we can step away and lighten the load. There's a letting-go required and a good deal of self-trust. Like everything involving growth and development, it's a process.

A woman has to believe:

> ➢ She can condense what she carries so that her backpack feels like it's feather-filled and has everything she needs.

> ➢ She can be true to her feelings without being overly emotional and out of control.

> ➢ She can remain *attached to the personal*, in tune with her values, without getting trapped by self-indulgence and over-exposure.

Attachment to the Personal

Keys to Becoming Un-Gagged

- Minimize the importance of what other people think.

- Find ways to understand the source of out-of-control emotions.

- Take pride in your depth of feelings and commitment.

- Avoid overload so you can move ahead freely.

- Be self-loving.

⌀ The Voice of Authority

Hillary Clinton, who many women consider as the role model for the voice of authority, has spent most of her adult life between a rock and a hard place.

> "She's too soft."
> "She's too hard."
> "I don't trust her."
> "She's not genuine."
> And so on…

She's probably the most qualified person who ever ran for President of the United States yet, as a woman, no matter what she did, she was damned if she did and damned if she didn't. We'll never know how she would have been characterized for the identical choices and behaviors if she'd been a man. And we can never know how each of us would be seen if we each did and said exactly what we're doing and saying, if we were men.

🗝 Quote:

> *"… I challenge assumptions about women. I do make some people uncomfortable, which I'm well aware of, but that's just part of coming to grips with what I believe is still one of the most important pieces of unfinished business in human history - empowering women to be able to stand up for themselves."*
>
> **Hillary Clinton (Vogue Magazine, 2009)**

For women in the workplace, the voice of authority begins with this proclaimed goal of women "standing up for themselves" and with being heard. The voice of authority also encompasses standing up for others, and more than that, it means inspiring and leading people to achieve what's new and better. As more and more women move into leadership roles in the workplace, in the government, and in the military, the models of leadership are evolving. Each woman must find her way to leadership through the path that fits her best. There's no single formula that will work for all.

The Women's March, the day after the U.S. presidential inauguration in January of 2017, marked a huge turning point in women's history and in women standing up for themselves and each other. As a result of one grandmother's Facebook post, an estimated 5 million people – including all genders, ages, ethnicities and socio/economic/cultural heritages – from all 50 states, 82 countries and 7 continents – from Antarctica to New Zealand, participated in denouncing the authority and authenticity of the newly inaugurated president, announcing to the world the voice of authority of women everywhere.

The 2017 election and The Women's March up-ended the view of the voice of authority, of the role of women in leadership and of leadership altogether. When the occupant in the White House is sending out stream-of-consciousness Tweet-storms, exposing his ego, contradicting himself daily, and fabricating unsubstantiated stories, the call to claim and defend the principles of leadership is screaming to be heard and restored.

Let's begin by examining traditional leadership roles.

It's easy to look to the military model for an unquestioned expression of authority. The number of women in military leadership roles is growing. According to the Pew Research Center, between 1973 and 2017, the percentage of women enlisted in the U.S. military increased from 2% to 14% and the percentage of female commissioned officers rose from 4% to 16%. Leadership in the military is certainly more clearly delineated than in the non-military world of work.

In the Harvard Business Review article, *"Leadership That Gets Results,"* Daniel Goleman tells us that the military "command" style of leadership in a non-military environment will have a negative effect on a work environment over time. The military model of leadership is never defied. It's an effective leadership strategy in times of emergency, crisis, or immediacy, where decisive leadership must be followed to avoid disaster. Goleman's research shows there is damage to the climate of a work environment through long-term use of this type of leadership approach. Even when a woman becomes a leader through military service, her authority must be developed beyond military demands and requirements.

Goleman's article shows the blending of the characteristics of Emotional Intelligence with six distinct leadership styles. The authoritative inspirational leader who mobilizes people toward a vision and who motivates people by communicating, "Come with me." has the most success as a leader. This style of leadership also includes the Emotional Intelligence characteristics of self-confidence and empathy and of being a change-agent who leads people in a new direction. This type of inspirational leader has the most strongly positive impact on a work environment.

This leadership article is a tiny spec in a huge universe of vastly informative sources that can also be overwhelming and intimidating, particularly to the new female leader.

Women in leadership positions (especially new leaders) often make mistakes based on resolutely believing that:

- ✗ They must be authoritarian and dogmatic or no one will take them seriously.
- ✗ They should change their nature so people will see them as an important figure and not take advantage of them.
- ✗ They can no longer socialize or be friendly with the people who used to be their coworkers.
- ✗ People who were formerly their peers won't like them anymore or will be jealous of them.
- ✗ Respect comes with the new leadership title. Their authority will be 100% recognized immediately.

These beliefs will damage a woman's ability to be heard. People will tune out and turn away. People will lose respect.

The following perspectives would be much more advantageous:

- ✓ The more considerate and open I am, the more buy-in and respect I'll get in return.

- ✓ The truer I remain to my basic nature, the more believable and real I'll come across to other people.
- ✓ The more I socialize with my old colleagues, the more in touch I'll be with their concerns and the more receptive they'll be to keeping me informed.
- ✓ Leadership is about respect and admiration. Popularity can't be my driver. Focusing on how people feel about me is detrimental.
- ✓ It's essential to build rapport, get to know people, gather information, and gain buy-in, before making changes in office configuration, job descriptions, and work roles. Respect must be earned; it's never automatic.

Damaging Enthusiasm

As the new Director of Career Services at a university, I was ready to make exciting changes to the open workspace. The Dean of Students had given me carte blanche to design and lay out my turf which was adjacent to and included two other departments sharing one administrative assistant. On my first day in my new job, I spent two evening hours rearranging furniture, with members of the custodial staff. There was plenty of space for all the various components I wanted to add and I knew the Dean of Students would be thrilled that the new service areas he'd hired me to provide were physically set up and in place so quickly.

The only person's desk I moved to a new location was the Administrative Assistant's desk, because it would be essential for her to greet and monitor students as they arrived for Career Services appointments or research help. I was excited about the configuration of everything. It had turned out even better than I'd pictured it in my mind.

The next day when I arrived, I could tell something was bothering the Admin. She and I had met briefly the day of my first interview and she'd been very pleasant the day before, although we hadn't sat down to talk one-on-one about the new Career Services Department I was hired to establish.

When I asked her to go for a coffee with me that second day, so we could get to know each other and talk about the roll-out and what her role would be, she gave me an icy look and claimed she had several urgent demands on her time that day and maybe tomorrow would be better. She ended up avoiding me completely for three days.

I realized too late that even though she knew I'd been hired to set up the new department and had been told I could use the space any way I wanted, she was insulted, hurt, and angry I hadn't talked to her before barging in and doing it so quickly. She had worked there for almost twenty years for two professors who asked her to do almost nothing. Her desk had always been tucked back in the corner out of the traffic flow and she loved to read her romance novels out of sight of the serious elite academic sages (as she described them to me many months later).

She knew all the ins and outs of everything that went on in that University; she knew the people to call for any need that came *up. She wasn't big on heavy-lifting kinds of demands or on project coordination which would have been quite appreciated. She did have a good attitude and liked being helpful. It took a long time for me to see the good side of her because she stayed angry at me for a long time.*

At some point, we finally became friendly. She eventually told me she thought every choice I'd made about how the furniture was placed was excellent and exactly the same placement she would have chosen, including the new location of her desk.

I'd been given the voice of authority when I walked in the door. I was young and enthusiastic and never thought what it would feel like for her to arrive at work and find her desk in a totally different location without anyone letting her know in advance. As far as she was concerned, I had abused my authority.

The simplest of interactions and a minimum of patience would have avoided the totally unnecessary debacle I encountered there. I had to pay the price for my lack of sensitivity. If I'd waited a day to sit down with her to ask for her input about what to move and where to move it, those first few months would have been much easier.

⚷ Reminder:

> ***Getting people's input and preferences about decisions and planning is beneficial and respectful, even if the decisions that follow are completely different from what they suggested.***

The voice of authority is on a higher plane than simple leadership. When you have established your voice, earned the respect of others, and have a devoted following, you can use your authority as a platform of righteous indignation for the causes that matter. It's critical to keep your emotions calmed and your voice tone free from anger to give full importance to the source of your vigilance. An explosion of feelings can take you off kilter and diminish the importance of your message and authority. The extreme expression of emotion can do more harm to your cause than benefit.

The voice of authority incorporates so many of the assets women naturally have, many that we've carefully looked at together. The voice of authority is a responsibility we all share and we must continue to aspire to. The voice of authority, more than ever, is a reflection and demonstration of many attributes:

The Voice of Authority

- compassionate and empathetic
- free from bias, racism and prejudice
- inspirational, motivating
- integrity/code of ethics, honest
- mutually respectful (at all levels)
- open, receptive, non-judgmental
- self-confident and self-assured
- values equality and diversity
- visionary change agent
- well-informed

The Importance of Female Trail Blazers

To find your voice of authority, look to the best examples around you. Seek out the women you admire, the women who lead, the women who lead wisely and strongly. There's much we can take from the wisdom of selected men as well. It's important, though, to guard against those grand male inflated voices behind the curtain like in *The Wizard of Oz*.

For all those women who beckon us on, who've spoken up and spoken out, showing us the voice of authority; for all those women who've had the courage to speak truth to power,

From Shirley Chisolm to Hillary Clinton

From Madonna to Beyoncé

From Eleanor Roosevelt to Michelle Obama

From Margaret Sanger to Gloria Steinem

From Golda Meir to Sonia Sotomayor

We thank you! We honor you! We emulate you!

We carry the torch.

The Voice of Authority

Keys to Becoming Un-Gagged

- Authority has to be earned.

- Your enthusiasm can blind you to other people's wishes.

- Ask for buy-in before making decisions that impact others.

- Emotional outbursts can be damaging to important causes.

- Aspire to blaze new trails; shine the light for those to follow.

It's A New Day

Jill just celebrated her 31st birthday. The twins, Hannah and Harry, turned one, the week before. She'd hoped they would have been born on her anticipated due date which was her 30th birthday. Not only were they born a week early; they also arrived in the prior month. Jill thought, "Good for them! They get their own day and their own month too."

Matt can't believe the metamorphosis that unfolded for Jill during her pregnancy and year of motherhood. He can feel the balance that Jill has achieved and he's a happy husband, a happy dad, and a happy camper!

Jill loves it that she and Matt are finishing each other's sentences again, like they did in college and when they were first married, and talking endlessly about everything from parenting to politics, from challenges at work to a demanding mother-in-law, from "Game of Thrones" to Yankee games.

When she learned she was expecting twins, Jill was terrified that she and Matt would lose their rekindled connection. What unfolded instead was the tightest of bonds, a tag team, loving the excitement and challenge, determined to take home a medal, as if they were in an Olympian competition.

Jill had shared with Matt many of the insights, new perspectives, and strategic approaches she'd gained from GAGGED. He was thrilled for her and most appreciative of how these simple basics had opened the door for her to gain balance and feel successful at work. Best of all, it laid the foundation for them to reconnect and re-find their marriage. Matt had eventually read GAGGED too. He said it added so much to his understanding and appreciation of Jill's challenges.

Jill often remarked how much she valued the many changes in her life. It felt as if she'd uncovered her true self and at the same time had let go of the many demands her true self had put on her. She was free. She was accepting. She was released from restraints and newly in tune with her core values.

The night before her birthday, she'd browsed through her well-worn copy of GAGGED while Matt was bathing the twins. She felt as if she were checking off the boxes of a to-do list. It was wonderful to recognize how she'd incorporated everything she was reading. The tenets of GAGGED had become second nature to her.

She saw how well she'd alleviated mistakes that had kept her from being heard at work and felt suddenly aware that through GAGGED she'd discovered valued principles to live by, to keep her life in balance, and to achieve success at work and at home. The sense of satisfaction she felt was quite different from the anxiety she was experiencing two years prior. She took a couple of deep long cleansing breaths.

After she closed the book and put it back in the top drawer of the night table, she rummaged through the drawer underneath, looking for her old journal which she'd written in daily, religiously, for many years and somehow stopped doing long before she and Matt got married.

She'd forgotten she'd written on almost every page and had never bothered to buy a replacement journal. One night in bed,

Matt had said to her, bathed in candlelight, in that charming old studio apartment they lived in back then, "I'll be your journal; you can whisper all your hidden secrets in my ear. They'll always be safe with me."

Jill immediately started writing on the last empty page of her journal. It felt satisfying to see how much insight and growth she'd gained as she wrote out her own sixteen guiding principles for a successful life.

It was quite freeing to realize she no longer felt gagged.

The Guiding Principles for a Successful Life

1. Accept what is; acknowledge what is beyond your control.
2. Be a sponge rather than a fly swatter; LISTEN!
3. Bring passion to what you do; give with your whole heart.
4. Commitment is required for success; stay engaged.
5. Experience gratitude; express appreciation.
6. Good communication is the key to solutions; validate people.
7. Inspire rather than impose.
8. Keep honesty and responsibility in all that you do.
9. People matter; connect with others; always find compassion.
10. Receive rather than judge; find common values.
11. Redefine success; incorporate feedback into new goals.
12. Reject blame, whining, seeking approval, apologetic groveling.
13. Remember that drive and motivation go beyond talent and smarts.
14. Seek gender freedom and respect.
15. Strive for balance; breathe into calm.
16. Unlock the quiet voice of authority; downplay the megaphone.

If you enjoyed reading **Gagged**, I would appreciate your recommending it to others and especially would be quite pleased if you would write a brief review on Amazon.

To receive detailed step by step Negotiation and Decision-Making grids to help you define your goals and make better decisions, go to:
TodaysEmpoweredWoman.com/Be-Heard

To receive a detailed step by step Development Plan template, incorporating your strengths and development areas, go to:
TodaysEmpoweredWoman.com/Be-Heard

To receive the Top Ten Tips for Receiving Feedback and the Top Ten Tips for Giving Feedback, go to:
TodaysEmpoweredWoman.com/Be-Heard

CHAPTER KEYS REVIEW

⌀ The Good Girl and the Cookie

Keys to Becoming Un-Gagged

- Feedback is always valuable.
- Managing your career means being proactive.
- It's up to you to promote your accomplishments.
- Confidence is magnetic and attracts people to you.
- Taking initiative is as important as conscientiousness.

⌀ The Impossible Ideal

Keys to Becoming Un-Gagged

- We are often our own barriers to success.
- It's important to understand where our basic beliefs come from.
- It's up to you to define your own ideals.
- Stereotypes are based in common beliefs.
- Recognizing the source of ambivalence can lead to clarity.

⌀ The Syndrome of Apology

Keys to Becoming Un-Gagged

- See yourself on equal footing with others.
- Become aware of and eliminate repetitive speech patterns.
- Look for ways to communicate without subservience.
- Save apology for when you've done something wrong.
- Communicate as a peer without asking for permission.

✒ Mechanics of Whining

Keys to Becoming Un-Gagged

- Learn to appreciate how multi-layered our voices are.
- Enrich your life by having strong role models.
- Remember how important nonverbal communication is.
- Make developing your voice a high priority.
- Practice deepening your voice's pitch to eliminate whining.

✒ Forgetting to Listen

Keys to Becoming Un-Gagged

- Empathy provides a foundation for Emotional Intelligence.
- Email, texting and social media are diluting communications.
- Women benefit from avoiding flowery emotional language.
- Listening attentively to validate people is a good goal.
- It's essential to challenge the myths we secretly tell ourselves.

✒ Conscientiousness to the Extreme

Keys to Becoming Un-Gagged

- Monitor the demands you put on yourself to avoid burnout.
- Remember the importance of demonstrating initiative.
- Be the one who speaks up for what's important to you.
- Make sure people are aware of your dedication.
- Bring balance and responsibility to your career management.

✒ The Imposition of Standards:

Keys to Becoming Un-Gagged

- Avoid thinking you can impose your standards on others.
- Make it a goal to inspire people to embrace a strong work ethic.
- Be the best role model you can be.
- Ask open-ended questions to encourage meaningful dialog.
- Know that people see you differently from your self-image.

✒ The Vicious Cycle: Feedback, Guilt and Defensiveness

Keys to Becoming Un-Gagged

- Our impact may be different from our intent.
- Guilt is a destructive overlay to productive process and action.
- Defensiveness is a barrier to growth and learning.
- A development plan is an excellent way to maximize feedback.
- It's valuable to make feedback an integral part of your life.

✒ Attachment to the Personal

Keys to Becoming Un-Gagged

- Minimize the importance of what other people think.
- Find ways to understand the source of out-of-control emotions.
- Take pride in your depth of feelings and commitment.
- Avoid overload so you can move ahead freely.
- Be self-loving.

✒ The Voice of Authority

Keys to Becoming Un-Gagged

↦ Authority has to be earned.

↦ Your enthusiasm can blind you to other people's wishes.

↦ Ask for buy-in before making decisions that impact others.

↦ Emotional outbursts can be damaging to important causes.

↦ Aspire to blaze new trails; shine the light for those to follow.

REMINDERS REVIEW

🗝 **Reminder:**

> *A coach, mentor, or prior coworker may be beneficial as you work on new communications. Feedback is always valuable. We cannot hear or see ourselves the way others do.*

🗝 **Reminder:**

> *Make sure you link the rewards you're seeking to benefits to the company (such as boosting morale, increasing productivity, enhancing efficiency, achieving better results, and/or gaining dedication to standards).*

🗝 **Reminder:**

> *We must make sure we're striving for our own ideals and not those we're unconsciously brainwashed to fit into.*

🗝 **Reminder:**

> *Instead of asking for permission, create communications where you are informing people.*

🗝 **Reminder:**

> *Research tells us that tone of voice is one of the two biggest components of how communication is received.*
> *(The other is facial expression.)*

🗝 Reminder:

> There's a way to express care and support for others genuinely without coating the communication in emotions.
>
> There's great advantage for women to express viewpoints and observations without wrapping them in emotional language.

🗝 Reminder:

> An important key to good workplace communication and to a woman's being heard, respected and appreciated, is through validated listening, expressed in rational unemotional language.

🗝 Reminder:

> Listening requires engagement.
>
> Listening is reflected by validation.
>
> Validation is different from agreement.

🗝 Reminder:

> Conscientiousness can be a passive attribute that diminishes initiative.

🗝 Reminder:
> Avoid using phrases like
> "I can't" "I have to" "There's no way I can"
> Avoid passive victimized language.

🗝 Reminder:
> The antidote for duality is balance.

🗝 Reminder:
> Train yourself to hear and experience what's being said as <u>information</u> only.
> <u>Learn</u> from feedback rather than <u>feel</u> from feedback.

🗝 Reminder:
> Women are about connection.

🗝 Reminder:
> There is no baggage-free ride in life.

🗝 Reminder:
> Getting people's input and preferences about decisions and planning is beneficial and respectful, even if the decisions that follow are completely different from what they suggested.

www.ingramcontent.com/pod-product-compliance
Lightning Source LLC
LaVergne TN
LVHW051600080426
835510LV00020B/3060